AT THE POND

David M. Schwartz *is an award-winning author of children's books, on a wide variety of topics, loved by children around the world.* Dwight Kuhn's *scientific expertise and artful eye work together with the camera to capture the awesome wonder of the natural world.*

For a free color catalog describing Gareth Stevens Publishing's list of high-quality books and multimedia programs, call 1-800-542-2595 (USA) or 1-800-461-9120 (Canada). Gareth Stevens Publishing's Fax: (414) 225-0377.

Library of Congress Cataloging-in-Publication Data

Schwartz, David M.
    At the pond / by David M. Schwartz; photographs by Dwight Kuhn.
        p. cm. — (Look once, look again)
    Includes bibliographical references (p. 23) and index.
    Summary: Examines the life in and around a pond, including bullfrogs,
crayfish, and snapping turtles.
    ISBN 0-8368-2244-7 (lib. bdg.)
    1. Pond animals—Juvenile literature. [1. Pond animals.]
I. Kuhn, Dwight, ill. II. Title. III. Series: Schwartz, David M.
Look once, look again.
QL146.3.S37   1998
591.763—dc21   98-6310

This North American edition first published in 1999 by
Gareth Stevens Publishing
1555 North RiverCenter Drive, Suite 201
Milwaukee, Wisconsin 53212 USA

First published in the United States in 1997 by Creative Teaching Press, Inc., P. O. Box 6017, Cypress, California, 90630-0017.

Text © 1997 by David M. Schwartz; photographs © 1997 by Dwight Kuhn. Additional end matter © 1999 by Gareth Stevens, Inc.

Printed in the United States of America

1 2 3 4 5 6 7 8 9 03 02 01 00 99

AT THE POND

by David M. Schwartz

photographs by Dwight Kuhn

A SPRINGBOARDS INTO SCIENCE SERIES

Gareth Stevens Publishing

MILWAUKEE

This insect has enormous eyes.
Some people think it is as scary as a dragon.

A dragonfly won't hurt you
unless you are as small as a bug.
Each enormous eye has
thousands of tiny lenses.
With its sharp eyesight,
a dragonfly sees flying
insects and catches
them in midair.

Cats do not live in ponds,
but this pond plant looks
like the tail of a cat.

It is called a cattail. In spring, it is covered with tiny yellow flowers. The flowers make yellow pollen.

The pollen helps make seeds, so new cattails can grow next year.

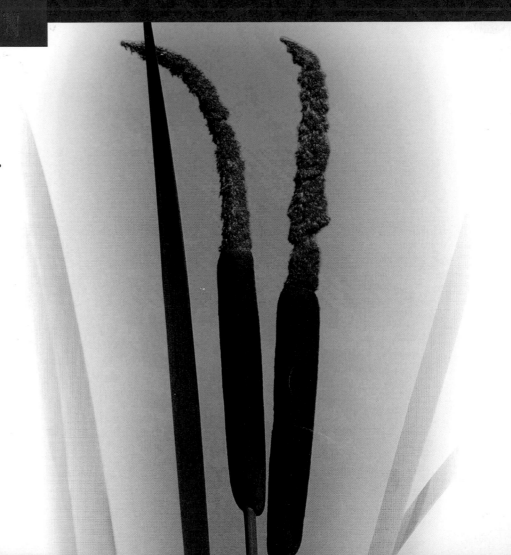

Whose webbed feet help it swim
quickly away when it is in danger?

It is a bullfrog. Bullfrogs are the largest frogs.
A bullfrog's bulging eyes search for flying insects.

Zap! A long, sticky tongue shoots out.
The bullfrog has a tasty treat.

These little bones are sharp to touch and nasty to taste.
Without them, this pond creature could not swim.

A sunfish has many fins. The fins on its back help it swim straight. Without these fins, it might turn over and over. It would not travel very far.

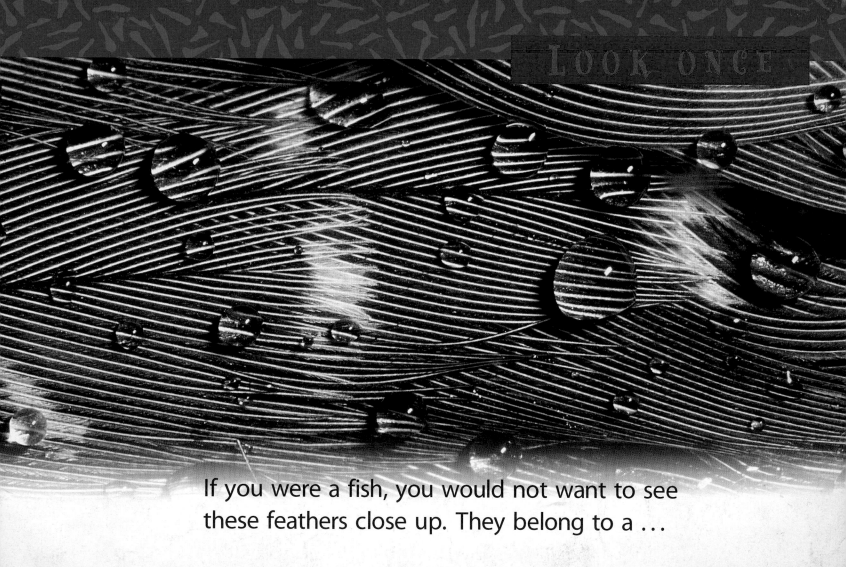

If you were a fish, you would not want to see these feathers close up. They belong to a ...

...kingfisher!
A kingfisher sits on branches or wires, looking for fish in the water below.

Its feathers are covered with oil to make them waterproof. A kingfisher stays dry while it eats a fishy meal.

This is not a bird, but it has
a beak. You do not want
this animal to snap at you!

Snapping turtles are fierce hunters. Their sharp jaws rip the flesh of fish, ducks, muskrats, or anything else that swims by. Make sure you don't get too close to a snapping turtle.

When these babies grow up, they will look like little lobsters. But lobsters live in the sea, not in a pond. These are ...

...crayfish babies. They cling underneath their mother's tail. Crayfish have many names. They are also called crawfish, crawdads, crawdaddies, crawcrabs, and mudbugs.

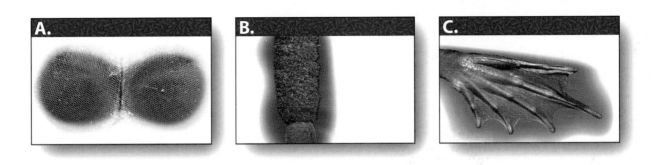

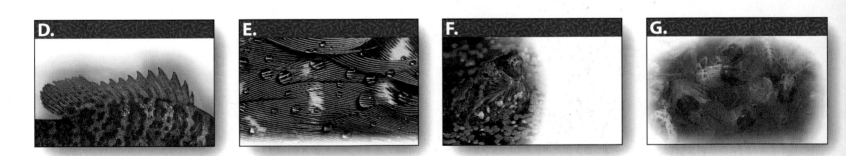

Look closely. Can you name these plants and animals?

A. Dragonfly

B. Cattails

C. Bullfrog

D. Sunfish

E. Kingfisher

F. Snapping turtle

G. Crayfish

How many were you able to identify correctly?

bulging: swelling or sticking out, like the eyes of a bullfrog.

bullfrog: the largest type of frog. It has a deep, hollow croak.

cling: to stick to or to hold tightly.

crayfish: a pond animal that looks like a small lobster. Crayfish belong to a group of animals called crustaceans.

enormous: very large; huge.

fins: the thin, flat parts that stick out from the body of a water animal. Fins are used for movement and balance.

flesh: the soft, meaty parts of an animal's body.

jaws: bony structures that hold the teeth in place and form the shape of the mouth.

lens: the part of the eye that focuses light rays.

midair: in the middle of the air. Dragonflies catch insect meals in midair.

muskrat: a furry animal with a long, scaly tail and waterproofed fur that lives in or near water.

pollen: tiny, usually yellow, grains of a flower that help produce seeds. Some people are allergic to the pollen of certain plants.

waterproof: able to keep water from coming through, like the oil-covered feathers of a kingfisher.

webbed: formed with a connecting fold of tissue, like the feet of ducks, frogs, and other animals that live in or near water.

Make a Pond Net

Make a pond net from a pair of old tights. Thread a thick piece of wire through the waist of the tights. Twist the ends of the wire together and tape them securely onto a long stick. Cut the legs off the tights. With a rubber band, attach a plastic margarine tub to the bottom of the tights. Collect some pond water with the net. Examine the water with a magnifying glass. After studying any life-forms, return the little creatures to the pond where you found them.

Get a Clear View

You can make your own underwater viewer with common household materials. Cut the top and bottom off a clean half-gallon milk carton (the waxy cardboard kind). Stretch some plastic wrap tightly over one end of the carton, and keep it snug with a rubber band. Practice using your viewer in a sink or bathtub. Then take it to a pond for some outdoor investigations. Be very careful, and always have an adult with you.

Two Words in One

The word *cattail* is a compound word, which means that it is made up of two smaller words — *cat* and *tail*. Make a list of all the compound words you find in this book. Play a game by writing the parts of these and other compound words on cards. Mix the cards up and try to put the compound words back together again.

A Colorful Fish

Fold a large sheet of paper in half. Draw a fish shape on the paper, then cut out the fish going through both layers of paper. Make lots of large fish scales from colorful tissue paper and glue the scales to your fish. Tape the fish sides together and add stuffing to the inside.

More Books to Read

Crustaceans. Fish. Frogs. Secrets of the Animal World (series). (Gareth Stevens)
Dragonflies. The New Creepy Crawly Collection (series). Heather Amery (Gareth Stevens)
Life in a Pond. Allan Fowler (Childrens Press)
Look Out for Turtles. Melvin Berger (HarperCollins)
Plant Communities: Where Can Cattails Grow? Herbert H. Wong (Addison-Wesley)
What's Under That Shell? A Book About Turtles. D. M. Souza (Carolrhoda Books)

Videos

Babies of the Pond. (Grunko Films)
The Pond. (Agency for Instructional Technology)
Pond and Puddle Life Through a Microscope. (Hatch, Warren Productions)
A Visit to a Pond. (Journal Films & Video)

Web Sites

www.teleport.com/~dstroy/froglnd.shtml
www.utexas.edu/depts/tnhc/.www/crayfish/pages/gallery.html

Some web sites stay current longer than others. For further web sites, use your search engines to locate the following topics: *bullfrog, cattail, crayfish, dragonfly, kingfisher, pond,* and *turtle.*